Holiday Pies

and

Tarts

HOLIDAY PIES
and
TARTS

HAMLYN

First published in 1997
by Hamlyn
an imprint of Reed International Books Limited
Michelin House, 81 Fulham Road, London SW3 6RB
and Auckland, Melbourne, Singapore and Toronto

ISBN 0 600 59356 8

Printed in Singapore

Publishing Director: Laura Bamford
Senior Editor: Sasha Judelson
Editor: Heather Thomas
Assistant Editor: Katey Day

Art Director: Keith Martin
Senior Designer: Louise Leffler
Design Manager: Bryan Dunn
Designer: Ginny Zeal

Photographer: Allan Rosenberg
Associate Photographer: Allen V. Lott
Food and Prop Stylist: Heidi Gintner
Prop Stylist: Sandra Griswold
Assistant Food Stylist: Kim Konechy
Production Controller: Dawn Mitchell

Notes

1 Use whole milk unless otherwise stated. 2 Use sweet (unsalted) butter unless otherwise stated.

Contents

Holiday Pies and Tarts

PIES AND TARTS *make delicious desserts for every occasion, from informal family gatherings to parties and holiday weekends. As the recipes featured in this book demonstrate, the number and variety of fillings, flavorings, and toppings is infinitely varied. You can fill pies and tarts with fresh, cooked, or puréed seasonal fruit, dried and candied fruits, ground nuts and even vegetables, such as pumpkin or sweet potato. Popular flavorings include coffee, chocolate, ground spices, and the grated zest and juice of lemons, oranges and limes.*

However, many people still worry about baking pies and prefer to buy ready-made pie crust dough in their local market rather than make it themselves. Making a crisp, flaky pie crust is a skill, and you need to be confident and light-handed to achieve successful results. Follow our expert advice and you cannot go wrong.

The right ingredients

Flour

Most pie crust recipes specify all-purpose or whole wheat flour, or a mixture of the two. Whole wheat flour makes a heavier pie crust and absorbs more liquid during mixing. Ideally, the flour should always be sifted to remove any lumps and to introduce more air into the mixture. Occasionally, self-rising flour is recommended in a recipe but it tends to produce a pie crust with a softer, more cake-like texture.

Fat

Butter, margarine, lard, or vegetable shortening are usually used. Whichever you choose, the fat should be at room temperature (unless otherwise specified in the recipe) as this makes it easier to rub into the flour. Pie crust made with butter is very crisp with a good flavor, whereas margarine gives a more flaky texture. Lard makes the most flaky pie crust but it is more suited to savory pies and quiches.

Liquid

Cold water is usually used for mixing the rubbed-in mixture of flour and fat to a pliable dough. Never add all the liquid at once—always add a little at a time, mixing between each addition until you get the desired texture. The dough should not be too wet nor too dry. Too much water produces a hard, tough pie crust, whereas too little water will make the dough tear and crack.

The golden rules for successful pie crust

I Stay cool

When making pie crust, you should insure that all the ingredients and your hands are as cool as possible. If your hands are too warm, the fat may become soft and oily and you will end up with crumbly pie crust. The best surface for rolling out the dough is a cold slab of marble, if you have one, but wood is perfectly adequate.

2 Handling the mixture

When rubbing the fat into the flour, use only your fingertips. Pie crust does not respond well to heavy handling and a light touch is essential. As you rub in the fat, lift small pieces into the air above the bowl and then lower your fingertips back down into the flour again. This helps introduce more air into the mixture and makes a lighter pie crust. Do not over-handle the mixture at this stage, nor the dough when you are rolling it out. The less you handle it, the better the pie crust will be!

3 The right mix

When all the fat is thoroughly rubbed into the flour and the mixture looks crumbly—like fine bread crumbs—you can add a little cold water, about a tablespoon at a time. The dough should be soft but not sticky, nor too dry. If it is too wet, add a little flour; if it is too dry, add some more cold water. Use a round-bladed knife to mix in the water, and always make sure that all the water is thoroughly mixed in.

4 Resting the dough

Although you can roll out the dough immediately, it is best to let it rest for 20–30 minutes first. This gives the gluten in the flour time to react with the water and become more elastic, easier to roll, and less likely to crack. Wrap the ball of dough in a plastic bag and leave it in the refrigerator. Chilling the dough helps prevent shrinkage.

5 Rolling out the dough

Roll out the dough gently but firmly on a lightly floured work surface—this will help prevent the dough sticking. Dust the rolling pin with flour beforehand, too. Remember to roll the dough slightly larger than the pie dish or pan you are using. It can be trimmed to fit when in place.

6 Cutting out shapes

If you are making small pies or tartlets, you can either cut them out with a cookie cutter or by cutting round an inverted saucer or plate with a sharp knife. If using a cutter, dip it in flour first, then place it on the dough and press down firmly. Do not twist it, or you will distort the shape.

7 Lining the pan

To transfer the dough to the prepared pie plate or pan, simply place the rolling pin under one end of the rolled-out dough, then gently roll the dough around it. Lift the rolling pin over one side of the pan and unroll to cover the pan. Press the dough down gently into position and then trim the edges neatly. If there are any cracks, you can patch them with any leftover dough trimmings. At this stage, you can, if wished, chill the lined pie pan in the refrigerator. This helps reduce shrinkage during baking and helps the dough to maintain its shape.

8 The right temperature

The temperature will vary from moderate to hot (usually 400°–450°F), according to the individual recipe and the type of pie crust used, but the oven should always be preheated to the correct temperature before baking the pie. Sometimes the temperature is reduced after 10 or 15 minutes for the remainder of the cooking time.

Equipment

You don't need any really expensive items of equipment for making pies and tarts. Of course, you can make the pie crust dough in a food processor, which saves some time, but the texture and finished result will not be as good as making it the traditional way by hand.

Pie pans

Metal pie pans, tart pans, and pie plates are best as they conduct heat better than glass or ceramic dishes and pans, giving you a really crisp pie shell. Some pans have loose removable bases, making it easier to turn out the pies.

Muffin and tartlet pans

You can buy fluted metal tartlet pans for making small pies and tartlets. Regular muffin pans can be used instead.

Rolling pins

These are usually wooden but they can be made of hollow heavy-duty glass or plastic, then filled with cold water to keep the pie crust dough cool when rolling it out. Top chefs favor heavy, long, cylindrical ones without handles.

Pastry brushes

These brushes are useful for oiling pans, and brushing the edges of the pie with a little water before pressing them together and sealing them. They can also be used for brushing the pie with milk or a beaten egg glaze prior to cooking, for a crisper, more golden finish.

Pastry crimpers

These are not essential but can be used to crimp the edges of a pie to create an attractive finish. Alternatively, you can use the blunt handle of a kitchen knife or the tines of a fork.

Wire racks

A hot pie, fruit tart, or a baked pie shell can be cooled quickly by removing it carefully from a pie pan with a removable base, and then placing it on a wire rack.

Prebaking the pie shell

It is often a good idea to bake the pie shell before adding the filling. This helps to avoid an under-baked base, insuring the base will be crisper and more appetizing. Simply line the pan with pie crust dough in the usual way, prick the base with a fork, then crumple up some waxed paper or kitchen foil and place it in the center of the pie. Fill with baking or dried beans and bake in a moderate to hot oven for 10–15 minutes. Remove the paper and beans, and return the pie shell to the oven for 5–10 minutes, just long enough to dry out the base and lightly color the edges of the pie shell. The time and temperature will vary, depending on whether the pie filling will require cooking.

Decorations for pies and tarts

There are many ways of decorating pies and tarts. Fresh fruit, piped cream, chocolate shavings, shreds of citrus zest, or chopped nuts make an attractive finish for fruit tarts and pies filled with an uncooked mousse mixture. Alternatively, you can try one of the following ideas.

Pie crust leaves

Use the leftover dough trimmings to cut out leaf shapes for decorating a pie. Use a sharp knife to make veins on them, and then fix in place with a little beaten egg. Brush with more egg glaze for a really golden brown finish.

Pie crust roses

Alternatively, you can use the trimmings to make a decorative rose for the top of the pie. Just cut a very long thin strip from the edge of one side of a rectangular piece of dough. Roll up to form the center of the rose, and then cut out some petals from the remaining trimmings. Fix them in position with beaten egg and arrange on top of the pie or bake separately and place over the steam-hole in the center of the pie crust before serving.

Lattice covering

Instead of covering a pie with a top layer of pie crust, you can cut the dough into thin strips and then lay them across the filling in a crisscross lattice pattern. Try twisting the strips to create a more unusual finish.

Glazes and sugar

An old-fashioned apple pie or any pie with a top crust can be made to look more appetizing by brushing it with milk, water, or beaten egg and then sprinkling with sugar before baking. This will produce a really crisp, flaky finish. You can dredge the cooked pie with more sugar, if wished.

Chocolate caraque

This makes an attractive decoration for many pies, tarts, and cakes. You can use good quality semi-sweet, milk, or white chocolate. To make chocolate caraque, break 4 oz of your chosen chocolate into small pieces and place them in a bowl over a saucepan of simmering water, until melted. Stir until smooth and then pour onto a marble slab or some waxed paper. The chocolate should be about ¼ inch thick. Set aside until just set. Using a sharp knife, draw it across the sheet of set chocolate at a 45-degree angle, creating large curls of chocolate. Use as required.

Alternative toppings for pies

Of course, you can cover a filled pie shell with many different toppings, including a traditional British crumble mixture or some glossy, crisp meringue.

Types of pie crust

Several types of pie crust are featured in the recipes in this book. With the possible exception of puff pastry, they are all relatively quick and easy to make, but you can buy ready-made fresh or frozen versions if you are in a hurry. Dredging the pie crust with sugar or brushing it with beaten egg or milk means that the pie will turn a wonderful golden color.

Regular pie crust

This is the most basic pie crust and is made in the traditional way by rubbing the fat into the flour and then mixing it to a pliable dough with water.

Sweet pie crust

Sugar is added to a basic pie crust mixture to give the pie crust a sweeter flavor.

Pâte brisée

This rich, flaky-textured pie crust has a high butter content. It can be rolled very thinly and is often used as a shell for elegant tarts and tartlets.

Pâte sucrée

This rich, sweet pie crust is a variation on pâte brisée. It is made directly on the work surface rather than in a bowl and care must be taken when handling the dough as the high sugar content makes it very crumbly. Pâte sucrée is very sweet and crisp, with a cookie-like texture, making it the perfect pie shell for fruit tarts and tartlets.

Pâte sablée

This literally means "sandy pastry" and it is lighter and less rich than pâte sucrée and pâte brisée. The basic flour and butter mixture is enriched with eggs and sweetened with sugar.

Puff pastry

Most recipes for puff pastry are very time-consuming and it is often easier to use the ready-made sort instead. However, if you do have the time it is well worth the trouble as home-made puff pastry is the most delicious pie crust of all. Crisp and puffed-up with several wafer-thin layers, puff pastry makes a special pie shell or covering for many fresh fruit desserts. Instead of rubbing the fat into the flour, it is diced, layered, and then folded into the dough. This process of folding traps air between the layers, which turns to steam during baking and as it expands the pastry is forced to rise. When baking puff pastry, the oven must be very hot indeed, usually 450°F, and the pastry should be baked just above the center of the oven. If you have a fan oven, check the manufacturer's instruction manual for the adjusted temperature.

BASIC PIE CRUST

2 cups all-purpose flour
pinch of salt
½ cup butter or margarine
3 tablespoons water

1 Sift the flour and salt into a bowl. Cut the fat into small pieces and rub it thoroughly into the flour with your fingertips until the mixture resembles fine bread crumbs.

2 Add the water, a little at a time, mixing it in with a knife, until you have a ball of dough that leaves the sides of the bowl clean. Knead lightly on a lightly floured surface, then put the dough in a plastic bag and leave in the refrigerator or a cool place to rest for 20–30 minutes. Roll out the dough and use as required.

Makes 8 ounces basic pie crust dough
Preparation time: 10 minutes, plus resting

SWEET PIE CRUST

1½ cups all-purpose flour
3 tablespoons butter or margarine
3 tablespoons lard or shortening
2 tablespoons sugar
1–2 tablespoons water

1 Sift the flour into a bowl and rub in the fat with your fingertips until the mixture resembles bread crumbs. Stir in the sugar and enough water to make a firm dough.

2 Turn out the dough on to a lightly floured surface and knead lightly until smooth. Place in a plastic bag and leave to rest in the refrigerator or a cool place for 30 minutes before using.

Makes 1 pound sweet pie crust
Preparation time: 10 minutes, plus resting

PUFF PASTRY

4½ cups all-purpose flour
2 cups butter, cut into pieces
1¼ cups water, chilled
1 teaspoon lemon juice

1 Sift the flour into a bowl and, using your fingertips, rub in one-third of the butter. Add the water and lemon juice and mix into the flour, until you have a smooth, elastic dough.

2 On a floured surface, roll out the dough to a rectangle, about ½ inch thick. Mark the dough across into 3 equal sections, and spread the remaining butter over two-thirds of the dough, leaving a 1-inch margin at the edges. Fold the unbuttered third back over half of the buttered dough, then fold again to cover the rest of the butter. Seal the edges to trap the air by pressing them together with a rolling pin.

3 With one of the short folded sides facing you, roll out the dough to form a large rectangle (as before). Fold into 3 again, then rest for 15 minutes. Repeat this stage 4 more times, resting the dough for 15 minutes each time. Then roll out and use as required.

Makes 2½ pounds puff pastry
Preparation time: 30 minutes, plus resting

PÂTE BRISÉE

2½ cups all-purpose flour
1 cup butter, cut into ½-inch cubes
2 teaspoons sugar
pinch of salt
1 small egg, lightly beaten
1 tablespoon cold water

1 Put the flour in a mixing bowl and make a hollow in the center. Put the butter, sugar, and salt in the hollow and mix lightly with the flour. Add the egg and mix to a smooth dough, adding the water if necessary.

2 Place the ball of dough on a floured surface and flatten it with your hand. Fold in half, then in half again. Knead into a ball shape and put in a plastic bag. Leave in the refrigerator or a cool place for 1 hour before rolling out and using.

Makes 1¼ pounds pâte brisée
Preparation time: 10 minutes, plus resting

PÂTE SABLÉE

3 cups all-purpose flour
⅔ cup sweet butter, chopped into small pieces
½ cup sugar
2 eggs

1 Sift the flour into a mixing bowl and rub in the butter until the mixture resembles fine bread crumbs.

2 Beat the sugar and eggs together, then add to the flour mixture. Mix to a smooth ball of dough. Put in a plastic bag and rest in the refrigerator or a cool place for 30 minutes before using.

Makes 1½ pounds pâte sablée
Preparation time: 10 minutes, plus resting

PÂTE SUCRÉE

1½ cups all-purpose flour
pinch of salt
6 tablespoons sugar
6 tablespoons butter, cut into small pieces
3 egg yolks

1 Sift the flour and salt on to a clean surface and make a hollow in the center. Put the sugar, butter, and egg yolks in the hollow, and mix into the flour with your fingertips, until you have a smooth, pliable dough.

2 Put the dough in a plastic bag and rest in the refrigerator or a cool place for 30 minutes before using.

Makes 1 pound pâte sucrée
Preparation time: 10 minutes, plus resting

CRÈME PÂTISSIÈRE

2 eggs
6 tablespoons sugar
3 tablespoons cornstarch
1 cup milk

1 Beat the eggs and sugar until light and creamy, then beat in the cornstarch.

2 Heat the milk to simmering point, then stir into the sugar, egg, and cornstarch mixture. Return the mixture to the pan and place over low heat, stirring constantly until the mixture thickens.

3 Pour into a clean bowl, beat quickly, and then cool. Cover with a lid or some plastic wrap until required.

Makes 1¼ cups crème pâtissière
Preparation time: 15 minutes

BANOFFI PIE

Crumb Crust:
8 oz graham crackers
½ cup butter

Filling:
¾ cup butter
¾ cup sugar
1¼ cups evaporated milk
2 bananas
1 tablespoon lemon juice
⅔ cup heavy cream
1 oz semisweet chocolate, shaved

1 Crumb the graham crackers in a food processor or place them between 2 sheets of waxed paper and crush with a rolling pin. Melt the butter in a pan and stir in the crumbs.

2 Press the mixture evenly over the base and sides of a deep 8-inch round pie pan. Chill until firm.

3 Make the filling. Place the butter and sugar in a pan. Heat gently, stirring until the butter has melted. Stir in the evaporated milk and bring to the boil. Lower the heat and simmer for about 15 minutes, stirring occasionally, until the mixture becomes a caramel color. Pour into the crumb base, cool, then chill until set.

4 Slice the bananas and toss them in the lemon juice. Reserve one-quarter of the bananas for decoration and spread the rest over the filling. Beat the cream and spread over the top. Decorate with the reserved bananas and sprinkle with shaved chocolate.

Serves 6–8
Preparation time: 30 minutes, plus chilling time

BANANA FILO PIE

¼ cup sweet butter
8 large sheets filo pastry, thawed if frozen
3 firm ripe bananas
2 tablespoons golden raisins
1 tablespoon soft brown sugar
1 tablespoon dark rum
1 teaspoon grated lemon zest
¼ cup slivered almonds, toasted
confectioner's sugar, for dusting

1 Melt most of the butter in a small saucepan. Brush 1 sheet of filo pastry with the melted butter and top with a second sheet. Brush with butter and repeat twice. Keep the remaining filo pastry sheets covered with a damp cloth to prevent them drying out.
2 Arrange the bananas in a 9-inch circle in the center of the filo pastry. Top the bananas with the golden raisins, sugar, rum, lemon zest, and almonds and then dot with the remaining butter.
3 Place the remaining filo pastry over the top of the pie, brushing each sheet of pastry with melted butter. Using a fluted tart pan or plate for shape, cut around the pie—be sure to leave a ½-inch edge.
4 Brush with melted butter and bake in a preheated oven at 375°F for 25–30 minutes. Serve dusted with confectioner's sugar.

Serves 6
Preparation time: 20 minutes
Cooking time: 30–35 minutes
Oven temperature: 375°F

TREACLE TART

Pie Crust:
2¼ cups all-purpose flour
½ cup chilled butter, diced

Filling:
½ cup light corn syrup
2 cups fresh white bread crumbs
grated zest and juice of 1 lemon

1 Make the pie crust. Put the flour in a bowl, add the butter and rub in until the mixture resembles fine bread crumbs. Stir in enough cold water, about 3–4 tablespoons, to mix to a firm dough.
2 Knead the dough briefly. Roll out and line an 8-inch deep tart pan. Trim the edges. Make cuts around the rim at 1-inch intervals. Brush the edges with water, then fold each piece in half to form triangular shapes. Chill for 30 minutes if time permits.
3 Warm the syrup until liquid, remove from the heat and stir in the bread crumbs, lemon zest, and juice. Spread over the pie shell.
4 Bake in a preheated oven at 375°F for 30–35 minutes, until golden.

Serves 6
Preparation time: 20 minutes, plus chilling time
Cooking time: 30–35 minutes
Oven temperature: 375°F

TOFFEE APPLE PECAN TARTS

Pie Crust:
2¼ cups all-purpose flour
½ cup butter, diced
2 tablespoons sugar

Filling:
1 pound tart green apples, peeled, cored, and chopped
¼ cup sugar

Topping:
¼ cup butter
¼ cup soft brown sugar
1 tablespoon light corn syrup
½ cup pecan halves

1 Put the flour in a bowl. Add the butter and rub in with the fingertips until the mixture resembles fine bread crumbs. Stir in the sugar, add about 2 tablespoons of cold water, and then mix to a firm dough.

2 Turn out on to a lightly floured surface and knead briefly. Roll out the dough thinly and cut into 12 x 3-inch rounds. Line 12 deep muffin pans with the dough. Place a little crumpled kitchen foil filled with a handful of baking beans inside and bake in a preheated oven at 400°F for 15 minutes, until the pie crust is just starting to brown. Remove the beans and kitchen foil.

3 Place the apples in a pan with 1 tablespoon of water, cover tightly and cook gently until soft, about 5 minutes. Remove from the heat and stir in the sugar. If the apple sauce is too liquid, return to the heat and simmer for a few more minutes. Cool slightly.

4 Make the topping. Place the butter, soft brown sugar, and light corn syrup in a pan and heat gently, stirring until the butter has melted. Boil for 2–3 minutes, until thickened. Remove from the heat and stir in the pecans.

5 Fill the tartlet shells with apple sauce, then top with a little toffee pecan mixture. Return to the oven for 10–15 minutes, until bubbling. Cool in the pans for 5 minutes.

Makes 12
Preparation time: 25 minutes
Cooking time: 25–30 minutes
Oven temperature: 400°F

HOT CHOCOLATE PECAN TART

A rich dessert, grand enough for entertaining, combining the texture and flavor of pecans
with chocolate and maple syrup, served in a chocolate pie shell.

Pie Crust:
1½ cups all-purpose flour
2 tablespoons unsweetened cocoa powder
½ cup sweet butter
¼ cup sugar
2 egg yolks
4 tablespoons cold water

Filling:
¾ cup sugar
⅓ cup maple syrup
¼ cup sweet butter
1 teaspoon vanilla extract
3 tablespoons unsweetened cocoa powder
3 eggs
1¾ cups pecan halves, very lightly chopped

To serve:
crème fraîche
ground cinnamon or confectioner's sugar

1 Make the pie crust. Sift the flour and cocoa powder into a bowl. Add the butter, cut into small pieces, and rub in gently with the fingertips until the mixture resembles fine bread crumbs.

2 Add the sugar, egg yolks, and enough cold water to make a firm dough. Knead lightly, then wrap and chill for 30 minutes.

3 Roll out the dough on a lightly floured surface and use to line a 9-inch x 1-inch deep pie pan with a removable base. Trim off any excess dough around the rim.

4 Line the pie pan with waxed paper and fill with baking beans or dried beans. Bake in a preheated oven at 400°F for 10 minutes, then remove the paper and beans and bake for a further 5 minutes. Reduce the oven temperature to 325°F.

5 Make the filling. Put the sugar and syrup in a small saucepan and heat until the sugar dissolves. Remove from the heat and stir in the butter until melted. Let cool slightly, then stir in the vanilla extract, cocoa powder, and eggs.

6 Scatter the chopped pecans in the pie shell and pour over the syrup mixture. Bake for about 50 minutes, until just set. Serve sliced with spoonfuls of crème fraîche, sprinkled with cinnamon or confectioner's sugar.

Serves 10
Preparation time: 25 minutes, plus chilling
Cooking time: about 1 hour 5 minutes
Oven temperature: 400°F, then 325°F

CHOCOLATE MOUSSE TARTLETS

Do make sure you buy the best-quality unsweetened chocolate for these tartlets, as the flavor is crucial.

Pie Crust:
2¼ **cups all-purpose flour**
½ **cup chilled butter, diced**
¼ **cup sugar**
1 **egg, beaten**

Filling:
6 **oz unsweetened chocolate, broken into squares**
2–3 **tablespoons water**
1 **tablespoon sweet butter, diced**
1 **tablespoon brandy or Cointreau**
3 **eggs, separated**
confectioner's sugar, for dusting

1 Put the flour in a bowl, add the butter and rub in with the fingertips until the mixture resembles fine bread crumbs. Stir in the sugar, then add the egg and mix to a firm dough, adding a little water if necessary.

2 Turn the dough out on a lightly floured surface and knead briefly. Roll out and line 8 x 3-inch deep tartlet or muffin pans. Reroll the dough trimmings and line 2–3 more pans. Fill each with crumpled kitchen foil and place on a cookie sheet. Bake in a preheated oven at 400°F for 15 minutes, then remove the foil and return the tartlets to the oven for 5 minutes. Leave to cool.

3 Make the filling. Place the chocolate in a heatproof bowl. Add the water. Set the bowl over a pan of hot water and leave until the chocolate has melted, stirring occasionally.

4 Remove the bowl from over the water and stir in the butter until it has melted. Add the brandy or Cointreau. Stir in the egg yolks. Beat the egg whites in a clean bowl until they are stiff and dry, and fold into the chocolate mixture.

5 Spoon the mousse mixture into the tartlet shells, then transfer to the refrigerator for 2–3 hours, until set. Dust the tartlets lightly with sifted confectioner's sugar before serving. Serve cold.

Serves 10–11
Preparation time: 25 minutes
Cooking time: 20 minutes
Oven temperature: 400°F

CHOCOLATE VELVET PIE

This chocolate shortbread base is an interesting variation on traditional Scottish plain shortbread.

Shortbread:
1½ cups all-purpose flour
2 teaspoons unsweetened cocoa powder
½ cup sweet butter
2 tablespoons sugar

Filling:
4 teaspoons unflavored gelatin
3 tablespoons cold water
⅓ cup sugar
3 egg yolks
1 tablespoon cornstarch
2½ cups milk
2 tablespoons finely ground espresso coffee
12 oz semisweet chocolate, broken into pieces

To decorate:
1¼ cups heavy cream
chocolate caraque (see page 9)

1 Make the shortbread shell. Grease a loose-base fluted tart pan, measuring 8 inches across the base and 2 inches deep. Sift the flour and cocoa powder into a bowl. Add the butter, cut into small pieces, and then rub in to the mixture with the fingertips. Add the sugar and mix to a dough.

2 Using your hands, press the shortbread mixture into the base and up the sides of the pan in an even layer. Bake in a preheated oven at 350°F for 20 minutes. Leave the base to cool.

3 Make the filling. Sprinkle the gelatin over the water in a small bowl and leave to soak.

4 Beat the sugar with the egg yolks, cornstarch, and a little of the milk in a bowl. Bring the remaining milk to the boil with the coffee powder, then pour it over the egg mixture, whisking well.

5 Return the mixture to the saucepan and heat gently, stirring until thickened. Remove the pan from the heat and then beat in the gelatin until dissolved.

6 Add the chocolate and stir until it has melted. Leave to cool slightly, then pour the mixture into the pie shell. Chill for several hours in the refrigerator until firm.

7 Transfer the pie to a serving plate. Beat the cream until it is stiff enough to hold its shape. Swirl over the top of the pie and scatter generously with chocolate caraque.

Serves 10
Preparation time: 35 minutes, plus chilling
Cooking time: 20 minutes
Oven temperature: 350°F

COCONUT CREAM PIE

5 tablespoons sugar
3½ tablespoons all-purpose flour
pinch of salt
1 egg
1¼ cups milk
1 teaspoon vanilla extract
5 tablespoons flaked unsweetened coconut
1 x 8-inch cooked pie shell
1 tablespoon toasted coconut
⅓ cup heavy cream, whipped

1 Beat together the sugar, flour, salt, and egg. Heat the milk in a saucepan to just below boiling point and then, very slowly, beat it into the flour and egg mixture.

2 Pour the mixture back into the saucepan and cook over low heat, stirring constantly, until just boiling.

3 Remove from the heat and add the vanilla. Allow the custard to cool completely, then stir in the coconut and pour into the pie shell. Decorate toasted coconut and with piped whipped cream.

Serves 4–6
Preparation time: 5 minutes
Cooking time: 10 minutes

ALASKA CRUMBLE PIE

Crumb Case:
6 oz oat cookies
6 tablespoons butter

Filling:
3 egg whites
¾ cup sugar
1 cup raspberries
1 cup redcurrants or blueberries
2 pints vanilla ice cream

1 Crumb the oat cookies in a food processor. Alternatively, place them between 2 sheets of waxed paper and crush with a rolling pin. Melt the butter in a pan, add the crumbs, and stir well. Press the mixture evenly over the base and sides of a 9-inch pie pan and chill until ready to serve.

2 Beat the egg whites in a clean bowl until stiff and dry. Beat in 1 tablespoon of the sugar, then fold in the rest.

3 When ready to serve, fill the crumb case with fruit and add scoops of ice cream. Spread the meringue over the top, covering the filling completely. Bake in a preheated oven at 400°F for 5–8 minutes, until the meringue is golden. Serve immediately.

Serves 4–6
Preparation time: 15 minutes
Cooking time: 5–8 minutes
Oven temperature: 400°F

CHOCOLATE AND HAZELNUT MERINGUE PIE

Pie Crust:
1½ **cups flour**
6 **tablespoons sweet butter**
1 **oz semisweet chocolate, shaved**
¼ **cup confectioner's sugar**
1 **egg yolk**
1–2 **teaspoons cold water**

Filling:
6 **tablespoons cornstarch**
3 **egg yolks**
2 **tablespoons sugar**
1 **teaspoon vanilla extract**
2½ **cups milk**
6 **oz semisweet chocolate, chopped**

Meringue:
3 **egg whites**
¾ **cup sugar**
¼ **cup hazelnuts, toasted and finely chopped**
light cream, to serve

1 Make the pie crust. Sift the flour into a bowl. Add the butter, cut into small pieces, and rub it in with the fingertips.

2 Stir in the chocolate, sugar, egg yolk, and enough water to mix to a firm dough. Knead lightly, wrap and chill for 30 minutes.

3 Roll out the dough on a lightly floured surface and use to line a 9-inch loose-based tart pan set on a cookie sheet.

4 Line the pan with waxed paper and fill with baking beans or dried beans. Bake in a preheated oven at 400°F for 15 minutes. Remove the paper and beans and bake for a further 5 minutes.

5 Make the filling. Mix together the cornstarch, egg yolks, sugar, vanilla, and a little of the milk in a bowl. Bring the remaining milk to the boil in a saucepan. Pour over the egg mixture, stirring.

6 Return the mixture to the pan and cook for 2 minutes, stirring until thickened. Add the chopped chocolate and stir until melted. Pour the mixture into the pie shell.

7 Make the meringue. Beat the egg whites until soft. Gradually beat in the sugar, a little at a time, until the mixture is stiff and glossy. Stir the hazelnuts into the meringue.

8 Spoon the meringue over the pie, shaping peaks with the back of a spoon. Place under a preheated hot broiler for about 2 minutes, until the peaks are golden. Serve warm or cold with light cream.

Serves 8
Preparation time: 40 minutes, plus chilling
Cooking time: 25 minutes
Oven temperature: 400°F

VARIATION

CHOCOLATE AND ORANGE MERINGUE PIE

Use 7 oz chopped white chocolate in place of the semisweet in the filling, and omit the sugar. Replace the chopped hazelnuts in the meringue with the finely grated zest of 1 small orange.

PECAN AND GRAPEFRUIT PIE

For the best flavor, grind the nuts just before using. Ground nuts deteriorate rapidly once processed.
Ruby red grapefruit add a delicate decoration and fragrance to the pie. Add to the pie just before serving so the juices
do not soak into the filling. If they are not available, use regular grapefruit as an alternative.

½ **quantity Pâte Brisée (see page 13)**
⅔ **cup pecans, ground**
1 cup sponge cake crumbs
5 tablespoons sugar
⅔ **cup tablespoons milk**
2 eggs

To decorate:
1 ruby red grapefruit
12 pecans

1 Line an 8-inch tart pan with the pâte brisée dough.
2 Combine the ground pecans with the cake crumbs in a bowl.
Beat the sugar, milk, and eggs together in another bowl and stir
this mixture into the pecans and crumbs.
3 Pour the mixture into the pie shell.
4 Bake in a preheated oven at 375°F for 10 minutes. Remove from
the oven and leave to cool.
5 Peel the red grapefruit and divide into sections. Using a sharp,
pointed knife, carefully remove the pith from the sections, leaving
them whole.
6 Arrange the grapefruit sections in the center of the pie, and
decorate the edge with whole pecans.

Serves 6–8
Preparation time: 20 minutes, plus cooling
Cooking time: 40 minutes
Oven temperature: 375°F

PECAN PIE

Pie Crust:
2¼ cups flour
½ cup chilled butter, diced
2 tablespoons sugar

Filling:
½ cup Barbados sugar
4 tablespoons molasses
4 tablespoons light corn syrup
6 tablespoons butter, melted
I teaspoon vanilla extract
grated zest of I lemon
4 eggs, beaten
1½ cups pecan halves

I Make the pie crust. Put the flour in a bowl, add the butter and rub in until the mixture resembles fine bread crumbs. Stir in the sugar, then add enough cold water, about 3–4 tablespoons, to mix to a firm dough.

2 Knead the dough briefly on a lightly floured surface, then roll out and line an 11 x 7-inch shallow jelly roll pan. Chill the pie crust for 30 minutes, if time permits.

3 Make the filling. Mix the sugar, molasses, syrup, butter, and vanilla extract in a bowl. Stir in the lemon zest and beaten eggs and mix well. Chop half the pecans and add to the filling mixture. Pour into the prepared pie crust.

4 Arrange the remaining pecans over the top of the pie. Bake in a preheated oven at 350°F for 45–50 minutes, until the pie shell is golden brown and the filling has set. Leave to cool, then cut into squares to serve.

Serves 8–10
Preparation time: 25 minutes
Cooking time: 45–50 minutes
Oven temperature: 350°F

VARIATIONS

WALNUT AND ORANGE PIE

Replace the pecans with walnut halves and use the grated zest of 1 orange instead of the lemon.

CHOCOLATE AND PECAN PIE

Add 2 tablespoons sifted unsweetened cocoa powder to the filling mixture. Sprinkle 2 oz shaved chocolate over the cooked baked pie.

PLUM AND ALMOND TART

½ quantity Pâte Brisée (see page 13)
½ cup sweet butter
½ cup soft brown sugar
2 eggs
1 cup ground almonds
2–3 drops almond extract
1 tablespoon cornstarch
5 large plums, halved and pitted
1 tablespoon soft brown sugar,
for sprinkling
10 whole almonds, blanched

1 Roll out the pâte brisée dough on a floured surface and use to line an 8-inch tart pan with a removable base. Rest for 30 minutes, fill with crumpled waxed paper and beans and bake in a preheated oven at 400°F for 20 minutes. Remove the paper and beans.
2 Beat the butter and sugar. Gradually beat in the egg, fold in the almonds, almond extract, and cornstarch. Pour into the tart shell.
3 Sprinkle the cut surface of the plums with the sugar and arrange on top of the almond mixture, skin side downward. Place an almond in the center of each plum half.
4 Reduce the oven temperature to 375°F and bake for 35 minutes.

Serves 6–8
Preparation time: 25 minutes, plus resting
Cooking time: 25 minutes
Oven temperature: 400°F, then 375°F

PLUM AND MARSHMALLOW PIE

1½ cups whole wheat flour
pinch of salt
6 tablespoons lard and butter, mixed
in equal amounts and cut into pieces
2 tablespoons cold water
1½ pounds plums, pitted
4 oz marshamallows
¼ cup sugar
milk, to glaze

1 Place the flour and salt in a bowl. Add the fats and rub in until the mixture resembles fine bread crumbs. Add the water and mix. Knead until smooth on a lightly floured surface. Wrap and let rest.
2 Mix together the plums, marshmallows, and sugar. Pile into a 2½-pint pie dish.
3 Roll out the dough to 2 inches larger than the pie dish top. Cut off a 1-inch strip all round and use to line the edge of the dish. Brush the strip with water.
4 Lift the rest of the dough on to the pie, pressing the edges together to seal. Trim, then brush with milk.
5 Place on a cookie sheet and bake in a preheated oven at 400°F for 30 minutes, until golden brown. Serve warm.

Serves 6–8
Preparation time: 20 minutes
Cooking time: 20 minutes
Oven temperature: 400°F

ORANGE CHEESE TORTE

12 oz Pâte Brisée (see page 13)
1⅓ cups low-fat soft cheese
2 eggs, separated
grated zest and juice of 1 orange
½ cup sugar
2 tablespoons all-purpose flour
1 cup heavy cream

To decorate:
1 orange, finely sliced
5 tablespoons sugar
1 cup water

1 Line an 8-inch tart pan with a removable base with the pâte brisée dough and prick with a fork. Rest for 30 minutes. Fill with crumpled waxed paper and baking beans and bake in a preheated oven at 375°F for 15 minutes.

2 Beat the cheese, egg yolks, orange zest and juice, sugar, flour, and cream together.

3 Beat the egg whites until they form soft peaks. Fold them into the cheese mixture.

4 Pour the mixture into the tart shell. Reduce the oven temperature to 350°F and bake for 30 minutes.

5 Put the orange slices, unpeeled, in a pan. Sprinkle them with the sugar and add the water. Bring the liquid slowly to simmering point and allow to simmer for 15 minutes. Drain the orange slices on paper towels.

6 Arrange the slices in a ring around the top of the torte, pressing them down gently. Return the torte to the oven and bake for a further 15 minutes. Serve hot or cold.

Serves 6
Preparation time: 45 minutes, plus resting and cooling
Cooking time: 1 hour
Oven temperature: 375°F, then 350°F

SWEET POTATO PIE

It is important that the sweet potato purée is free from excess liquid or the filling will be too wet. Baking the sweet potatoes whole in the oven helps eliminate this problem.

Pie Crust:
1 cup all-purpose flour
6 tablespoons butter, chilled and diced
½ cup pecans, ground finely
3 tablespoons sugar
2–3 tablespoons cold water

Filling:
1 sweet potato, weighing about 12 ounces
2 large eggs, beaten
1 heaped tablespoon grated fresh ginger
1 cup heavy cream
½ cup soft brown sugar
½ teaspoon ground allspice
½ teaspoon vanilla extract
½ teaspoon salt

Meringue:
½ teaspoon ground cinnamon
¾ cup sugar
3 egg whites
pinch of salt

1 Start by preparing the sweet potoato for the filling. Scrub the unpeeled sweet potato well, prick all over 2 or 3 times with a fork and place on a cookie sheet in a preheated oven at 350°F for 40–45 minutes, or until tender. Remove from the oven and let cool. When cool enough to handle, peel the sweet potato and place the flesh in a large bowl. Mash well, then set aside.

2 To make the pie shell, sieve the flour into a bowl and add the butter. Rub the butter into the flour until the mixture resembles fine bread crumbs. Stir in the ground pecans and sugar, mixing in well. Add enough water to make a firm dough.

3 Roll out the dough on a lightly floured surface until about ¼ inch thick and use to line a 10-inch fluted pie pan. Place the lined pie pan in the refrigerator until ready to use.

4 Preheat the oven to 400°F and place a cookie sheet on the middle shelf of the oven.

5 Add the remaining filling ingredients to the sweet potato purée and mix well until smooth. Then pour the filling into the pie shell.

6 Cover the pie edge with a foil ring and place on the heated cookie sheet and bake for 25–30 minutes, until golden and the filling has almost set but the center is still a little wobbly. Remove the foil ring.

7 To make the meringue, mix the cinnamon with the sugar. Beat the egg whites with a pinch of salt until stiff but not dry, then beat in the cinnamon sugar, a spoonful at a time. Cover the surface of the pie with the meringue and return to the oven for 10–15 minutes until golden all over.

Serves 6–8
Preparation time: 20 minutes
Cooking time: 1–1¼ hours
Oven temperature: 350°F, then 400°F

PUMPKIN PIE

To make pumpkin purée, simply steam or boil the pumpkin chunks for 15–20 minutes until tender, then drain thoroughly. Purée in a blender or food processor or press through a sieve.

Pie Crust:
2¼ cups flour
½ cup chilled butter, diced
2 tablespoons sugar

Filling:
2 cups puréed cooked or canned pumpkin
2 eggs, beaten
⅔ cup light cream
⅓ cup soft brown sugar
1 teaspoon ground cinnamon
½ teaspoon ground ginger
¼ teaspoon ground nutmeg

To decorate:
⅔ cup heavy cream
ground cinnamon

1 Make the pie crust. Place the flour in a bowl, add the butter and rub in with the fingertips until the mixture resembles fine bread crumbs. Stir in the sugar, then add enough cold water, about 3–4 tablespoons, to mix to a firm dough.

2 Turn the dough out on to a lightly floured surface and knead briefly. Roll out and line a 9-inch pie plate. Gather up the leftover dough, reroll thinly, and cut into leaf shapes. Brush the edge of the pie crust lightly with water and attach the leaves.

3 Make the filling. Mix the pumpkin purée, eggs, cream, sugar, and spices in a large bowl. Pour into the pie crust and bake in a preheated oven at 375°F for 45–50 minutes, until the filling has set. Leave to cool.

4 To decorate the pie, beat the cream in a bowl until stiff. Spoon cream swirls around the edge of the pipe and sprinkle with a little ground cinnamon.

Serves 6–8
Preparation time: 25 minutes
Cooking time: 45–50 minutes
Oven temperature: 375°F

MERINGUE MINCE PIES

12 oz mincemeat
2 egg whites
½ cup sugar

Pie Crust:
1½ cups flour
½ cup whole wheat flour
½ cup chilled butter, diced
½ cup ground almonds
2 teaspoons grated lemon zest
¼ cup sugar
1 egg yolk
2–3 tablespoons orange juice

1 Make the pie crust. Put the flours in a bowl, add the butter, and rub in until the mixture resembles fine bread crumbs. Stir in the almonds, zest, sugar, and egg and enough juice for a firm dough.
2 Knead the dough on a floured surface. Roll out and stamp out 18 x 3-inch rounds. Use to line 18 muffin pans. Fill with mincemeat.
3 Beat the egg whites in a clean bowl until stiff and dry, then fold in the sugar. Pile a little of the meringue into each pie shell. Bake in a preheated oven at 375°F for 30 minutes, until golden brown .

Makes 18
Preparation time: 30 minutes
Cooking time: 25-30 minutes
Oven temperature: 375°F

CHOCOLATE PIE

4 oz semisweet or white chocolate, broken into pieces
2 teaspoons unflavored gelatin
3 tablespoons hot water
⅔ cup light cream

Pie Crust:
2 tablespoons sugar
3 tablespoons butter
2 eggs, separated
⅔ cup all-purpose flour

1 To make the pie crust, beat the sugar and butter until light and fluffy, then beat in 1 egg yolk. Gradually stir in the flour to a soft, pliable dough. Knead lightly, then roll out the dough to fit a 6-inch fluted tart pan. Prick with a fork and set aside for 30 minutes. Fill with crumpled kitchen foil and beans and bake in a preheated oven at 400°F for 15–20 minutes, removing the beans and foil for the last 5 minutes. Turn out on to a wire rack and cool.
2 Reserve 1 square of chocolate and melt the rest in a bowl over a pan of hot water. Remove from the heat and beat in the remaining egg yolk. Dissolve the gelatin in the hot water. Stir into the chocolate mixture, then stir in the cream. Cool until almost set. Beat the egg whites until soft peaks form, then fold into the mixture. Chill for 2 hours, or until set. Pile the mixture into the pie shell. Shave the reserved chocolate and sprinkle over the pie.

Serves 4–6
Preparation time: 15 minutes, plus 3 hours to rest and set
Cooking time: 15–20 minutes
Oven temperature: 400°F

33

MINCEMEAT AND TANGERINE PIE

Pie Crust:
¾ cup flour
¾ cup whole wheat flour
6 tablespoons chilled butter, diced
½ cup ground almonds
2 tablespoons sugar
grated zest of 1 orange
1 egg, beaten

Filling:
12 oz mincemeat
3 tangerines, peeled and divided into sections
confectioner's sugar, for dusting (optional)

1 Make the pie crust. Place the flours in a bowl, add the diced butter and rub in with the fingertips until the mixture resembles fine bread crumbs. Stir in the ground almonds, sugar, and orange zest, then add the beaten egg and up to 2 tablespoons of cold water, and mix to a firm dough.

2 Knead the dough briefly on a lightly floured surface, then roll out and line an 8-inch tart pan. Gather up the leftover dough, reroll, and cut into holly leaf shapes. Stick some of the holly shapes to the edge of the pie crust with a little water. Reserve about 6 holly shapes. Chill the pie crust in the refrigerator for 30 minutes, if time permits.

3 Mix the mincemeat and tangerine sections in a bowl; spoon the mixture into the pie shell. Arrange the reserved holly shapes over the top. Bake in a preheated oven at 400°F for 25–30 minutes, until the pie shell is golden brown. Dust with confectioner's sugar and serve warm or cold.

Serves 6
Preparation time: 20 minutes
Cooking time: 25–30 minutes
Oven temperature: 400°F

APPLE MERINGUE PIE

1 pound tart green apples,
peeled, cored, and sliced
⅔ cup sugar
2 tablespoons butter
grated zest of 1 lemon
⅔ cup water
2 eggs, separated
cream, to serve

Pie Crust:
1½ cups flour
pinch of salt
6 tablespoons butter
1½–2 tablespoons water

1 To make the pie crust, sift the flour and salt into a bowl. Add the butter, cut into small pieces, and rub in until the mixture resembles fine bread crumbs. Add enough water to form a firm dough. Knead the dough lightly until smooth and free from cracks.

2 Roll out the dough on a lightly floured work surface to a round large enough to line the base and sides of an 8-inch fluted pie pan with a removable base.

3 Line the pie shell with waxed paper and cover with a layer of baking beans. Bake in a preheated oven at 400°F for 10–15 minutes, until the sides of the pie crust are set and golden. Remove the paper and beans and return the pie shell to the oven for about 5 minutes, or until the base is crisp. Let the pie shell cool.

4 Put the apples in a saucepan with ¼ cup of the sugar, the butter, lemon zest, and water. Cook gently until the apples are tender, then beat to a smooth purée.

5 Cool the mixture slightly, then beat in the egg yolks. Spoon the mixture into the pie shell. Lower the oven temperature to 350°F and bake for 20 minutes.

6 Beat the egg whites until stiff, beat in the rest of the sugar, then spread the meringue over the top of the apples. Return to the oven for 15–20 minutes, until golden. Serve hot or cold with cream.

Serves 4–6
Preparation time: 25 minutes
Cooking time: 50–55 minutes
Oven temperature: 400°F, then 350°F

BLUEBERRY SHORTCAKE TART

Pie Crust:
3 cups self-rising flour
¾ cup chilled butter, diced
½ cup sugar
I egg, beaten
milk, see method

Filling:
2 cups fresh or frozen blueberries
2 tablespoons sugar
½ cup slivered almonds
cream or crème fraîche, to serve

I Put the flour in a bowl, add the butter and rub it in until the mixture resembles fine bread crumbs. Stir in the sugar, add the egg and mix to a firm dough, adding a little cold water, if necessary.

2 Roll out two-thirds of the dough and use to line a greased 9-inch tart pan. Spread the blueberries evenly over the tart shell and sprinkle with the sugar.

3 Roll out the remaining dough and cut into thin strips. Brush the rim of the tart with water and arrange the strips in a lattice pattern over the top. Brush the strips with a little milk and sprinkle with the slivered almonds.

4 Bake in a preheated oven at 375°F for 30–35 minutes, until the pie crust is golden and the blueberries are tender. Serve the tart warm or cold with cream or crème fraîche.

Serves 6
Preparation time: 25 minutes
Cooking time: 30–35 minutes
Oven temperature: 375°F

WINTER FRUIT PIE

This deliciously fragrant pie is perfect for serving when supplies of fresh fruit are limited. The filling is even better when made the day before to allow the fruit to plump up.

Pie Crust:
1½ cups whole wheat flour
1½ teaspoons baking powder
1 teaspoon salt
6 tablespoons chilled butter, diced
2 tablespoons sugar
beaten egg, to glaze

Filling:
1¼ cups red wine
1 strip of lemon zest
⅓ cup soft brown sugar
1 cinnamon stick
pinch of ground nutmeg
1 cup ready-to-eat pitted prunes
1 cup ready-to-eat dried apricots
6 oranges, peeled and divided into sections

1 Make the filling. Warm the wine in a saucepan with the lemon zest, sugar, and spices, stirring until the sugar has dissolved. Add the prunes and apricots, then simmer for 10 minutes, until the mixture is slightly thickened.

2 Stir the orange sections into the pan, then remove from the heat. Remove the lemon zest and cinnamon stick.

3 Make the pie crust. Put the flour, baking powder, and salt in a bowl. Add the butter and rub in with the fingertips until the mixture resembles fine bread crumbs. Stir in the sugar, then add enough cold water, about 3–4 tablespoons, to mix to a firm dough.

4 Turn the dough out on to a lightly floured surface and knead briefly. Spoon the filling into a 1½-pint deep pie dish and brush the edge of the dish with water. Roll out the dough to measure 2 inches larger than the dish. Cut off a 1-inch strip all round and press this strip on to the edge of the pie dish.

5 Dampen the dough edge lightly with water and cover the pie with the remaining dough, trimming off the excess. Press the pastry edges together to seal, then pinch to decorate. Roll out the leftover dough and cut out some leaf shapes. Attach these to the pie with a little water, then brush the pie with beaten egg.

6 Bake the pie in a preheated oven at 400°F for 30–35 minutes, until the pie crust is crisp and rich golden brown. Serve hot with cream or thick yogurt.

Serves 6
Preparation time: 35 minutes
Cooking time: 30–35 minutes
Oven temperature: 400°F

SPICED BRAMBLE PIE

11 oz blackberries, fresh or frozen
7 oz tart green apples, peeled, cored, and thinly sliced
juice of ½ lemon
½ teaspoon ground ginger
¼ teaspoon ground mace
½ teaspoon apple pie spice
⅓ cup soft brown sugar
11 oz prepared Puff Pastry dough (see page 12)
1 egg yolk, beaten

1 Mix all the ingredients except for the pastry and egg. Transfer to a 1½-pint pie dish. Roll the pastry 2 inches wider than the pie dish.
2 Cut a 1-inch band from the circumference of the rolled dough and use to cover the entire rim of the pie dish. Trim.
3 Brush the rim with water, then cover with the "lid" of dough. Trim the edges with scissors or a very sharp knife.
4 Press the edges together and flute them. Make a hole in the center of the pie to let the steam escape during cooking.
5 Decorate the top with trimmings. Brush with the egg yolk.
6 Bake for 20 minutes in a preheated oven at 475°F. Reduce the heat to 375°F and bake for 25 minutes. Watch the pie crust, you may need to cover it with a ring of foil after 15 minutes.

Serves 6
Preparation time: 20 minutes
Cooking time: 45 minutes
Oven temperature: 475°F, then 375°F

APRICOT TART

½ quantity Pâte Sablée (see page 13)
8 large fresh apricots, halved, reserve 4 pits
⅔ cup vanilla-flavored sugar
1 cup water
1 quantity Crème Pâtissière (see page 13)

1 Line an 8-inch tart pan with a removable base with the pâte sablée dough. Rest for 30 minutes. Fill with crumpled waxed paper and beans and bake in a preheated oven at 400°F for 15 minutes. Remove the paper and beans. Reduce the heat to 375°F and bake for 10 minutes. Remove the tart shell from the pan and cool.
2 Crack 4 of the apricot pits and remove the kernels.
3 Put the kernels, sugar, and water in a pan and simmer for 5 minutes. Add the apricots and poach for about 10 minutes, until tender. Drain on paper towels. Spread the crème pâtissière in the shell. Arrange the fruit on top.

Serves 6
Preparation time: 35 minutes, plus resting
Cooking time: 25 minutes
Oven temperature: 400°F, then 375°F

MANGO PUFF TARTLETS

8 oz prepared **Puff Pastry**
(see page 12)
1 ripe mango
2 tablespoons sweet butter
4 teaspoons sugar
2 tablespoons apricot preserve

1 Divide the puff pastry into quarters, and roll out each piece to a 4-inch round. Space the rounds on a greased cookie sheet.
2 Peel the mango and cut in half. Cut each half in half again. Slice the mango quarters thinly and arrange over the pastry rounds.
3 Dot some butter over each mango topping and sprinkle with the sugar. Bake in a preheated oven at 425°F for 12–15 minutes, until the pastry is risen and golden and the mango is tender.
4 Warm the apricot preserve in a small saucepan, press it through a sieve into a bowl, then carefully brush over the top of each mango tartlet. Serve the tartlets warm.

Makes 4
Preparation time: 10 minutes
Cooking time: 12–15 minutes
Oven temperature: 425°F

MANGO STAR PIE

1 pound prepared **Puff Pastry**
(see page 12)
2 ripe mangoes, peeled, halved and pitted
2 tablespoons lime juice
2 oz unsweetened dry coconut, minced
2 tablespoons soft brown sugar
beaten egg and sugar, to glaze

1 Roll out half the puff pastry dough to a 12-inch round. Make "V"-shaped cuts all round to form a star shape. Roll out the remaining dough to a 12-inch round and place the star-shaped dough on top. Using a sharp knife, cut the lower piece of dough to a star shape, using the upper piece as a guide.
2 Slice the mangoes thinly. Place one piece of dough on an oiled cookie sheet and arrange the mango on top to within ½ inch of the edges. Sprinkle with lime juice, coconut, and soft brown sugar. Brush the edges of the dough with water and cover with the remaining piece of dough. Press the edges together firmly to seal.
3 Brush with egg and sprinkle with sugar. Bake in a preheated oven at 425°F for 25 minutes, until risen and golden. Serve hot.

Serves 6
Preparation time: 20 minutes
Cooking time: 20–25 minutes
Oven temperature: 425°F

CRANBERRY AND ALMOND TARTLETS

Pie Crust:
1½ **cups all-purpose flour**
6 **tablespoons butter, diced**
2 **tablespoons sugar**
1 **egg yolk**

Filling:
½ **cup softened butter**
½ **cup sugar**
2 **eggs, beaten**
1 **cup ground almonds**
few drops of almond extract
2 **tablespoons all-purpose flour**
3 **tablespoons cranberry jelly**
1 **cup cranberries**
confectioner's sugar, for dusting

1 Put the flour in a bowl, add the butter and rub in with the fingertips until the mixture resembles fine bread crumbs. Stir in the sugar, add the egg yolk and about 2 tablespoons of cold water. Mix to a firm dough.

2 Turn out the dough on to a lightly floured surface and knead briefly. Divide into 4, then roll out each piece to line a 4-inch tartlet pan. Prick each base with a fork and chill for 15 minutes.

3 Make the filling. Beat together the butter and sugar until light and fluffy. Add the eggs, a little at a time, then add the almonds, almond extract, and the flour. Mix well.

4 Spread the cranberry jelly over the tartlet shells. Divide the almond mixture between the shells and smooth the tops. Sprinkle the cranberries over the top. Bake in a preheated oven at 375°F for 35–40 minutes, until the filling is risen and firm. Cool in the pans for 5 minutes, then dust the tops with confectioner's sugar and serve warm or cold.

Serves 4
Preparation time: 20 minutes, plus chilling time
Cooking time: 35–40 minutes
Oven temperature: 375°F

SPICED APPLE PIE

1½ pounds tart green apples, peeled, cored, and thinly sliced
⅓ cup soft brown sugar
1 teaspoon apple pie spice
4 cloves
1 quantity Basic Pie Crust (see page 12)
water and sugar, to glaze

Crème à la vanille:
2 egg yolks
1 teaspoon cornstarch
2 tablespoons sugar
1¼ cups milk
½ teaspoon vanilla extract

1 Layer the apples with the sugar and spices in a 1½-pint pie dish. Roll out the dough to a circle 2 inches larger than the dish. Cut a strip all round and use to cover the dampened rim of the dish; brush with water. Cut the dough into strips and make a lattice covering over the apples (see page 9), sealing the edges. Trim the edges, make a hole in the center. Brush with water, sprinkle with sugar, and bake in a preheated oven at 400°F for 30–40 minutes.
2 Make the crème à la vanille: cream the egg yolks with the cornstarch and sugar. Bring the milk to the boil, pour on to the egg mixture and stir. Heat gently, stirring until the mixture coats the back of a spoon. Add the vanilla, then strain. Serve with the pie.

Serves 4–6
Preparation time: 20 minutes
Cooking time: 30–40 minutes
Oven temperature: 400°F

DARTOIS AUX PÊCHES

2 large or 3 small fresh peaches
11 oz prepared Puff Pastry dough (see page 12)
1 egg, separated
3 tablespoons vanilla-flavored sugar

1 Drop the peaches into boiling water and leave for 45 seconds. Remove, then slip off their skins, and pit and dice them.
2 Roll out half the pastry to form an 8 x 6-inch rectangle. Transfer to a greased cookie sheet, lay flat and prick with a fork.
3 Brush with the egg white, then pile the peaches in the center, leaving a 1-inch margin at the edges. Sprinkle with the sugar.
4 Roll out the second half of the dough a little larger than the first and use to cover the peaches and the first piece of dough. Seal the edges well, then flute. Set aside for 20 minutes.
5 Brush with the egg yolk and bake in a preheated oven at 475°F for 15 minutes. Reduce the heat to 375°F and bake for 20 minutes.

Serves 8
Preparation time: 15 minutes, plus resting
Cooking time: 35 minutes
Oven temperature: 475°F, then 375°F

SPICED CHEESE TARTLETS

8 oz Basic Pie Crust (see page 12)
⅓ cup seedless raisins
¼ cup butter
¼ cup sugar
1 teaspoon finely grated lemon zest
1 large egg, lightly beaten
1 tablespoon self-rising flour
½ teaspoon ground cinnamon
1⅓ cups cream cheese, softened
2 tablespoons milk

1 Roll out the pie crust dough, then cut into 3-inch circles with a fluted cookie cutter and use to line 14-16 muffin pans. Lightly prick the dough with a fork and put a few raisins in the bottom. Beat the butter, sugar, and lemon zest until soft and light.
2 Gradually beat in the egg, then the flour sieved with the cinnamon, the cream cheese, and the milk. Divide the mixture between the tartlet shells. Bake in a preheated oven at 350°F for about 30 minutes, or until the filling is well risen and set.

Makes 14-16
Preparation time: 25 minutes
Cooking time: 30 minutes
Oven temperature: 350°F

CHEESE AND HONEY TARTLETS

1 quantity Pâte Sucrée
(see page 13)
1⅓ cups cream cheese, softened
3 tablespoons clear honey
grated zest of ½ orange
pinch of ground cinnamon
⅔ cup heavy cream, beaten until stiff

Topping:
2 cups blackcurrants or blueberries
4–6 tablespoons water
sugar, to taste

1 Roll out the pâte sucrée dough and line 8 x 4-inch tartlet pans. Fill with crumpled waxed paper and baking beans and bake in a preheated oven at 375°F for about 10 minutes. Remove the beans and paper and return to the oven to dry out for a few minutes. Cool on a wire rack. Roll out the leftover dough and cut into 8 or 16 leaf shapes, about 1 inch long. Bake on a lightly greased cookie sheet in the preheated oven for 7 minutes, until lightly browned.
2 Put the blackcurrants or blueberries in a pan with the water, cover, cook gently until tender. Sweeten to taste and leave to cool.
3 Beat the cream cheese until smooth, then beat in the honey, orange zest, and cinnamon. Fold in one-third of the cream. Divide the mixture between the tartlet shells. Spoon over the blackcurrant or blueberry mixture. Pipe the remaining cream on to the tartlets. Decorate with the pie crust leaves.

Makes 8
Preparation time: about 45 minutes
Cooking time: about 20 minutes
Oven temperature: 375°F

CRANBERRY AND APPLE ALMOND PIES

Pie Crust:
6 tablespoons all-purpose flour
½ cup chilled butter, cut into pieces
½ cup ground almonds
¼ cup sugar
3–4 tablespoons cold water

Filling:
6 tablespoons butter
½ cup sugar
I large egg, beaten
¼ cup all-purpose flour
I cup ground almonds
4 crisp, tart dessert apples, peeled, cored, and cut into thick slices
I cup fresh or frozen cranberries, defrosted if frozen

Glaze:
I teaspoon butter
I teaspoon sugar

To serve:
confectioner's sugar and heavy cream

1 To make the pie crust, sift the flour into a bowl and add the butter. Rub the butter into the flour until the mixture resembles fine bread crumbs. Stir in the ground almonds and sugar, mixing in well. Add enough water to make a firm dough.

2 Roll out the dough on a lightly floured surface until about ¼ inch thick and use to line 4 x 5-inch fluted pie pans.

3 Preheat the oven to 400°F and place a cookie sheet on the middle shelf.

4 To make the filling, beat the butter and sugar until light and fluffy, then beat in the egg with a spoonful of the flour. Add the remaining flour with the ground almonds and mix well. Spoon a quarter of the mixture into each pie shell and spread out evenly.

5 Arrange the apple pieces from 1 apple on top of each pie, pushing them lightly into the filling. Scatter each pie evenly with the cranberries. Melt the butter and then brush over the pies. Sprinkle some sugar over each pie and place on the heated cookie sheet. Bake in the preheated oven for 15 minutes, then reduce the temperature to 350°F and continue baking for 20-30 minutes, until the filling has set and is golden all over. Lightly sift over with confectioner's sugar and serve the pie warm or cold with cream.

Serves 6–8

Preparation time: 20 minutes
Cooking time: 35–45 minutes
Oven temperature: 400°F, then 350°F

VARIATION

CRANBERRY AND APPLE ALMOND PIE

To make a whole pie, arrange the ingredients in a 10 inch fluted pie pan and bake in a preheated oven at 375°F for 40–45 minutes.

APPLE AND ORANGE TART

1 quantity Sweet Pie Crust (see page 12)
2 pounds tart green apples, peeled, cored, and sliced
1 tablespoon water
¼ cup sugar
grated zest of 2 oranges
3 ruby red oranges

Glaze:
4 tablespoons apricot preserve
2 tablespoons water
1 teaspoon lemon juice

To serve:
whipped cream

1 Roll out the sweet pie crust dough and use to line an 8-inch tart pan with a removable base. Line with waxed paper and baking beans and bake in a preheated oven at 400°F for 15–20 minutes. Remove the paper and beans and return to the oven for 5 minutes. Remove the tart shell from the pan and cool on a wire rack.

2 Place the apples in a saucepan together with the water and sugar. Cover and cook gently to a pulp, stirring occasionally. Cool slightly, then purée in a blender or food processor. Return to the pan and add the orange zest. Cook, uncovered, until thick, stirring occasionally. Leave until cool, then turn into the tart shell and smooth the top evenly.

3 Peel the oranges, removing all the pith. Slice thinly and arrange on top of the tart. Heat the apricot preserve with the water and lemon juice, then sieve and reheat. Brush over the oranges. Serve the tart with whipped cream.

Serves 6
Preparation time: 25 minutes
Cooking time: 20–25 minutes
Oven temperature: 400°F

APPLE AND ORANGE SPONGE TART

Pie Crust:
1½ cups all-purpose flour
6 tablespoons chilled butter, diced
1 egg yolk

Filling:
½ cup butter, softened
½ cup sugar
2 eggs
1 cup self-rising flour
grated zest and juice of 1 orange
3 small apples, peeled, cored, and quartered
2 tablespoons apricot preserve

1 Put the flour in a bowl, add the butter and rub in with the fingertips until the mixture resembles fine bread crumbs. Stir in the egg yolk and enough cold water, about 2-3 tablespoons, to mix to a firm dough.

2 Turn the dough out on to a lightly floured surface and knead briefly. Roll out and use to line a 9-inch deep tart pan. Chill in the refrigerator for 30 minutes.

3 Make the filling: combine the butter, sugar, eggs, flour, orange zest, and juice in a bowl. Beat together for 2-3 minutes until light and fluffy. Spread the mixture over the pie crust.

4 Slice each apple quarter thinly and fan out slightly. Place one in the center of the filling and space the rest out evenly around the edge of the tart.

5 Bake in a preheated oven at 375°F for 35–40 minutes, until the pie crust is golden and the filling set. Warm the apricot preserve in a saucepan, strain it into a bowl, then brush it over the top of the tart. Serve the tart warm or cold.

Serves 6–8
Preparation time: 20 minutes
Cooking time: 35–40 minutes
Oven temperature: 375°F

APPLE AND BERRY CRUMB PIE

Pie Crust:
1½ cups all-purpose flour
pinch of salt
6 tablespoons butter or margarine, cut into small pieces
1½–2 tablespoons water

Filling:
9 ounces apples, peeled, cored, and thickly sliced
1½ cups cranberries
⅓ cup sugar
1½ cups all-purpose flour
6 tablespoons butter
¾ teaspoon ground cinnamon
½ teaspoon grated lemon zest
⅓ cup soft brown sugar

Liqueur Cream:
1½ cups heavy cream
sifted confectioner's sugar, to taste
Cointreau, Grand Marnier, or other liqueur, to taste

1 To make the pie crust, sift the flour and salt into a bowl, add the butter or margarine and rub in until the mixture resembles fine bread crumbs. Add enough water to form a firm dough. Knead lightly until smooth and free from cracks.

2 Roll out the dough on a lightly floured surface to a round large enough to line the base and sides of an 8–9-inch loose-based fluted pie pan. Chill until required.

3 For the filling, toss the apples and cranberries with the sugar and put into the pie shell. Put the flour, butter, cinnamon, and lemon zest in a bowl, then rub together until crumbly. Stir in the soft brown sugar. Sprinkle evenly over the fruit and pat down lightly.

4 Bake in a preheated oven at 350°F for 45 minutes, or until the crumb topping and pie crust are golden brown.

5 To make the liqueur cream, beat the cream until it begins to thicken. Sweeten to taste with sifted confectioner's sugar and add a spoonful or two of Cointreau or other liqueur to taste, then continue beating until thick. Serve the pie warm or cold, with the liqueur cream.

Serves 6–8
Preparation time: 25 minutes
Cooking time: 45 minutes
Oven temperature: 350°F

TARTE TATIN

Pie Crust:
1½ cups all-purpose flour
6 tablespoons chilled butter, diced
2 tablespoons sugar
1 egg yolk

For the apples:
¼ cup butter
¼ cup sugar
6 apples, peeled, cored,
and sliced

1 Put the flour in a bowl, add the butter and rub in until the mixture resembles fine bread crumbs. Stir in the sugar. Add the egg and 2–3 tablespoons of water, to mix to a firm dough.
2 Prepare the apples. Melt the butter and sugar in an 8-inch skillet. When golden, add the apples and cook until caramelized.
3 Roll out the dough to a round, a little larger than the skillet. Place over the apples, folding under until it fits the skillet neatly.
4 Bake in a preheated oven at 400°F for 40 minutes, until golden.
5 Cool for 5 minutes, and then invert on to a plate.

Serves 4–6
Preparation time: 20 minutes
Cooking time: 35–40 minutes
Oven temperature: 400°F

LITTLE MARZIPAN AND APPLE PIES

milk, for brushing
1 tablespoon soft brown sugar (optional)

Filling:
7 ounces tart green apples, peeled,
cored, and coarsely chopped
3 ounces ready-made marzipan, cut into
¼-inch cubes

Pie Crust:
1 cup all-purpose flour
1 cup whole wheat flour
pinch of salt
½ cup hard vegetable margarine, diced
from the freezer
3–4 tablespoons water

1 To make the pie crust, put both the flours and salt in a large bowl. Rub the margarine gently into the flour, then add the water as necessary. Mix to a fairly firm dough, then put the dough into a plastic bag and chill in the refrigerator for 1 hour.
2 For the filling, mix the apples and marzipan together in a bowl.
3 Roll out the dough thinly. Cut out 12 rounds, using a 3-inch fluted cookie cutter, and 12 rounds, using a 2-inch fluted cookie cutter. Line 12 small muffin pans with the larger rounds and spoon the filling into them.
4 Brush both sides of the remaining rounds with milk and lay them on top of the tartlets. Press to seal and sprinkle with a little sugar.
5 Bake in a preheated oven at 425°F for 15–20 minutes. Remove from the pans and leave to cool slightly on a wire rack.

Makes 12
Preparation time: 25 minutes, plus chilling
Cooking time: 15–20 minutes
Oven temperature: 425°F

CHOCOLATE AND ORANGE BOSTON CREAM PIE

Boston cream pie is a two-layer cake with a pastry cream filling and chocolate frosting.

Cake:
2 cups self-rising flour
½ teaspoon salt
2 teaspoons baking powder
½ cup butter, softened
I cup sugar
finely grated zest of I orange
2 eggs, separated
⅔ cup fresh orange juice

Pastry Cream:
2 egg yolks
¼ cup sugar
3 tablespoons all-purpose flour
I cup milk
¼ teaspoon vanilla extract
I oz semisweet chocolate, chopped

Chocolate Frosting:
2 oz semisweet chocolate
¼ cup butter
⅓ cup confectioner's sugar
½ tablespoon orange-flavored liqueur
(optional)

I Preheat the oven to 350°F. Butter and lightly flour 2 x 8-inch round cake pans.

2 To make the cake layers, sift the flour, salt, and baking powder in a large bowl. In another bowl beat the butter, sugar, and orange zest together until light and fluffy, then beat in the egg yolks, one at a time, until well combined. Fold in the flour and orange juice in three stages, mixing well to combine.

3 Beat the egg whites until stiff but not dry. Stir one-third of the egg whites into the cake batter, then gently fold in the rest. Divide the batter evenly between the 2 cake pans and level the surface.

4 Bake in the oven for 30–35 minutes, until golden all over. Leave for 5 minutes in the pans before turning out on to a wire rack.

5 To make the pastry cream, beat the egg yolks and sugar in a bowl until almost white, then fold in the flour. Put the milk in a heavy pan and bring almost to the boil. Beat the hot milk into the yolks, sugar, and flour mixture and mix well.

6 Return to the pan and stir until it thickens and comes to a boil. Stir in the vanilla, pour into a bowl and sprinkle the surface lightly with a little sugar to prevent a skin from forming. Leave to go completely cold before stirring in the chopped chocolate.

7 To make the frosting, melt the chocolate, butter, and sugar in a heatproof bowl over a saucepan of hot but not boiling water, stirring occasionally (be careful that it does not overheat) until completely melted and smooth. Remove from the heat and stir in the orange liqueur, if using. Leave to cool and thicken slightly.

8 To assemble the pie, spread the pastry cream filling on one of the cake layers, place the remaining cake layer on top and pour the chocolate frosting over the top, letting it drip down the sides slightly. Keep refrigerated until ready to serve.

Serves 8
Preparation time: 30 minutes
Cooking time: 40–45 minutes
Oven temperature: 350°F

CHOCOLATE SWIRL TART

Crumb Shell:
6 tablespoons butter
4 ounces graham crackers
2 ounces amaretti cookies

Filling:
7 ounces semisweet chocolate
1¼ cups heavy cream

1 Melt the butter in a saucepan and then stir in the cracker and cookie crumbs. Press the mixture into a greased 9-inch pie plate. Leave to chill in the refrigerator until firm.
2 Place the chocolate in a heatproof bowl over a pan of hot, not boiling, water. Stir gently until melted. Cover a rolling pin with kitchen foil and brush lightly with oil. Drizzle a little chocolate on to the rolling pin in zigzag lines, about 1 inch long. Chill until set.
3 Beat the cream until stiff and fold into the remaining melted chocolate. Spoon into the crumb case and chill for 2 hours, until set.
4 Just before serving, carefully peel the chocolate decorations from the kitchen foil and pile into the center of the tart.

Serves 6–8
Preparation time: 20 minutes, plus chilling time

LEMON AND PASSION FRUIT PIE

Pie Crust:
1½ cups flour
½ cup butter, diced
2 tablespoons sugar

Filling:
4 eggs
½ cup sugar
⅔ cup heavy cream
finely grated zest and juice of 3 lemons,
preferably unwaxed

To decorate:
seeds from 3 passion fruit
⅔ cup heavy cream, beaten until just
holding its shape

1 Put the flour in a bowl, add the butter and rub in with the fingertips until the mixture resembles fine bread crumbs. Stir in the sugar, then add about 2 tablespoons of cold water and mix to a firm dough. Wrap in plastic wrap and chill for 15 minutes.
2 Roll out the dough and line an 8-inch fluted pie pan, trimming the dough. Line with waxed paper and fill with beans. Bake in a preheated oven at 400°F for 15 minutes. Remove the beans and paper and cook for a further 5 minutes. Reduce the oven to 325°F.
3 Make the filling. Beat together the eggs and sugar, then stir in the cream, lemon zest and juice. Pour into the pie shell and bake for 25–30 minutes, until just set. Leave to cool.
4 Stir the seeds of 2 passion fruit into the cream, then spoon over the pie. Sprinkle with the remaining seeds and serve within 1 hour.

Serves 8
Preparation time: 25 minutes, plus chilling time
Cooking time: 40–45 minutes
Oven temperature: 400°F, then 325°F

PEAR TARTS

Make sure the pears are thoroughly poached and tender, otherwise they will brown once sliced. Drain thoroughly.

½ **quantity Pâte Brisée**
(see page 13)
½ **bay leaf**
1 clove
slice of lemon zest
1¾ cups water
⅔ cup sugar
3 pears, weighing 14 oz, peeled,
halved, and cored
1 quantity Crème Pâtissière
(see page 13)

1 Roll out the pâte brisée dough on a lightly floured surface and use to line 6 x 4-inch loose-based tart pans. Rest for 30 minutes. Line with crumpled waxed paper and baking beans and bake in a preheated oven at 400°F for 20 minutes. Remove the beans and paper and bake for a further 5 minutes. Cool.

2 Put the bay leaf, clove, lemon zest, water, and sugar in a pan. Stirring continuously, heat gently over low heat.

3 When the sugar has dissolved, add the pears and poach until tender, about 10 minutes.

4 Remove the pears from the syrup and drain on paper towels, then slice thinly almost to the stem end, but keep attached to the stem. Reserve the liquid.

Spread the crème pâtissière over each tart shell, then arrange a pear half on top, in a fan shape.

5 Boil the syrup rapidly until thick, then brush over the pears. Remove the tarts from the pans and serve immediately.

Serves 6
Preparation time: 30 minutes, plus resting
Cooking time: 35 minutes
Oven temperature: 400°F

BUTTERSCOTCH MERINGUE PIE

Pie Crust:
I cup flour
6 tablespoons chilled butter, diced
2 tablespoons sugar
½ cup ground hazelnuts
I egg yolk

Filling:
6 tablespoons cornstarch
½ cup soft brown sugar
1¼ cups milk
¼ cup butter, diced
3 egg yolks
I teaspoon vanilla extract

Meringue:
3 egg whites
¾ cup sugar

I Make the pie crust. Put the flour in a bowl, add the butter and rub in with the fingertips until the mixture resembles fine bread crumbs. Stir in the sugar, ground hazelnuts, and then add the egg yolk and enough cold water, about 2–3 tablespoons, to mix to a firm dough.

2 Knead the dough briefly on a lightly floured surface, then roll out and line an 8-inch pie pan. Chill for 30 minutes, if time permits, then fill with crumpled kitchen foil and bake in a preheated oven at 400°F for 15 minutes. Remove the foil and bake the pie shell for a further 5 minutes.

3 Combine the cornstarch and soft brown sugar in a pan. Blend in the milk until smooth. Heat gently, stirring until thickened, then cook for 1 minute. Cool the sauce slightly. Beat in the butter, a few pieces at a time, then stir in the egg yolks and vanilla. Pour the filling into the pie shell.

4 Whisk the egg whites in a clean bowl until they are stiff and dry. Whisk in 1 tablespoon of the sugar, then fold in the rest. Spread the meringue over the filling to completely enclose it.

5 Return the pie to the oven for 10 minutes, or until the meringue is golden. Serve warm or cold.

Serves 6
Preparation time: 35 minutes
Cooking time: 30 minutes
Oven temperature: 400°F

TOFFEE APPLE PIE

¼ **cup butter**

1½ **pounds apples, peeled, cored, and sliced**

¼ **cup soft brown sugar**

juice of 2 oranges

2 **tablespoons brandy or Calvados**

12 **oz prepared Puff Pastry (see page 12)**

beaten egg, to glaze

1 Melt the butter in a skillet, add the apples and fry all over for about 10 minutes, until just starting to brown. Stir in the sugar, orange juice, and brandy and allow the mixture to bubble for a few minutes, until it forms a thick syrup. Remove from the heat and leave to cool.

2 Roll out half of the puff pastry dough on a lightly floured surface and line a 9-inch pie pan. Fill with apple mixture and brush the pie crust edges with water. Roll out the remaining dough and use to cover the pie. Pinch the edges of the dough together to seal. If liked, mark a zigzag pattern on top of the pie with a knife, taking care not to cut through the dough.

3 Brush with beaten egg. Bake in a preheated oven at 425°F for 25–30 minutes, until golden.

Serves 6

Preparation time: 20 minutes
Cooking time: 25–30 minutes
Oven temperature: 425°F

LEMON MERINGUE TART

Pie Crust:
1½ cups flour
6 tablespoons chilled butter, diced
2 tablespoons sugar
½ cup ground hazelnuts
1 egg yolk

Filling:
6 tablespoons cornstarch
½ cup sugar
1¼ cups water
grated zest and juice of 2 lemons
3 egg yolks

Meringue:
3 egg whites
¾ cup sugar

1 Make the pie crust. Put the flour in a bowl, add the butter, and rub in until the mixture resembles fine bread crumbs. Stir in the sugar and ground hazelnuts, then add the egg yolk and enough cold water, about 2–3 tablespoons, to make a firm dough.

2 Knead the dough briefly on a lightly floured surface, then roll out and line an 8-inch tart pan. Chill for 30 minutes, then fill with crumpled kitchen foil and baking beans and bake in a preheated oven at 400°F for 15 minutes. Remove the kitchen foil and beans and bake the tart shell for a further 5 minutes.

3 Mix the cornstarch and sugar in a saucepan. Add the water, lemon zest and juice, and stir until well blended. Bring to the boil, stirring until thickened and smooth. Cool slightly.

4 Beat the egg yolks in a bowl, then beat in 2 tablespoons of the lemon sauce. Return this mixture to the pan and cook gently until the sauce has thickened further. Pour the sauce into the tart shell.

5 Beat the egg whites in a clean bowl until stiff and dry. Beat in 1 tablespoon of the sugar, then fold in the rest. Spread the meringue mixture over the tart shell to completely cover the filling. Return to the oven for 10 minutes, until the meringue is golden. Serve the tart warm or cold.

Serves 6
Preparation time: 35 minutes, plus chilling time
Cooking time: 30 minutes
Oven temperature: 400°F

INDEX